MW00892718

Copyright © 2018 by Khadizhat Witt

circumwanderers@gmail.com

This book is dedicated to my daughter Aya who started traveling the world when she was 6 weeks old, and to my husband Justin who makes these travels possible.

Summer vacation has begun!

Nick and Aya are helping their mother to pack for a new trip. Their father George is an environmentalist and his next assignment is to explore some remote places in the biggest country of the world, so the family will combine his work with their vacation. This time they are flying to Russia.

A plane takes them on a 10 hour-long flight from New York to Moscow, crossing over the Atlantic Ocean and Northern Europe. Moscow is the capital and largest city in Russia.

The next morning Nick and Aya are ready to explore the city. "I've heard that Moscow has a famous square with red walls, buildings and towers. I want to see it," declares Aya.

The family arrives at Red Square and the first thing that attracts the kids' attention is Saint Basil's Cathedral. "It looks like a castle from a fairy tale!" exclaims Aya. "Look at all the colors and the domes! I have to go around and count them!"

"The clock on the tower is so big! What is behind the fortified walls? Can we go inside?" asks Nick. "Later today, we are going on a tour and will explore palaces, cathedrals and take a closer look at the Kremlin towers," responds George. "The Kremlin is the official residence of Russia's President."

In the evening the family tries Russian cuisine for dinner. They all eat PIROZHKI, which resemble the empanadas they had tried in Argentina. Aya likes the BORSCHT soup and OLIVIER potato salad. Kate especially enjoys the MEDOVIK honey cake for desert.

Over the next few days, the family takes a cruise on the Moscow River followed by a walk on the Arbat, a street that has existed since at least the 15th century. They visit the Pushkin Museum of Fine Arts, where Nick creates his own art while Aya listens to children's stories written by the Russian poet Alexander Pushkin.

After Moscow, they take a short flight to Saint Petersburg and check into a hotel near the River Neva flowing through the city. In the past, Saint Petersburg was the capital of Russia and is still home to numerous palaces, parks, museums, and monuments.

They go to the
Hermitage Museum
on the first day of
their stay.

The family takes a day trip to Peterhof Palace, that was built in the early 1700s by Peter the Great, the Emperor of Russia at that time.

The favorite activity of the kids is counting fountains. Aya counts 45 of them, but Nick really wants to find out how many she missed. He reads in a brochure that there are over 200 statues and 144 fountains in the area of the Peterhof Park.

The next day is full of explorations in Pushkin, a suburb of Saint Petersburg. "This is another big palace! Who lives here?" asks Aya. "Nobody lives here now," responds her mother, "It is a museum. Back in the 18th century, it was the summer residence of Catherine the Great who ruled Russia at that time. Let's go inside and see the famous Amber Room."

"Wow! We are in a real treasure room, which I have seen only in cartoons before now. Look at all the sparkles! I don't want to leave!" shouts Aya.

"Come on Aya, I want to go feed squirrels
in the garden! They are very friendly!"
Nick waves his arms with excitement.

After visiting these current and former capitals of Russia, the adventurers fly to Sochi, a city located on the Black Sea. Sochi Park, an amusement park full of roller coaster rides and other entertainment, becomes Nick and Aya's new favorite place.

Throughout the week they splash in the Black Sea, ride a cable car to an Alpine resort called Rosa Khutor, and hike in the Caucasus Mountains. "I remember camping next to the Andes Mountains in Argentine Patagonia, and now we are seeing the beautiful nature of the Caucasus! Do you know that the highest mountain in Europe is here in Russia, not far from where we are now?" asks Nick. "You are right, the mountain you are talking about is called Elbrus. You know a lot about geography, son. I am very proud of you!" exclaims his dad.

From Sochi they fly to Kazan, the capital city of the Tatarstan Republic. "Some buildings look really different here," says Aya while pointing at the Kul Sharif Mosque as they drive by. "Tatarstan is a place where different cultures, religions, and traditions mixed throughout history. There are many people of different ethnic backgrounds here," explains Kate.

"Those buildings are amazing!" exclaims Aya as they enter the Kazan Kremlin. "What are they? Can we go inside?"

"Yes, we are going to visit this beautiful mosque which is called Kul Sharif. There are many mosques in the world, where people go to pray to the Creator they call Allah in their language," responds George.

"Dad, what does the crescent moon mean? And all these writings in a language I can't understand?" asks Nick.

"The crescent moon and the minaret towers, that you see there on the roof, represent the religion of Islam. Just like the domes and crosses are symbols of Orthodox Christianity," Nick's father explains, pointing first at the mosque and then at the church, which stand next to each other in the territory of the Kazan Kremlin, surrounded by fortified walls. Suddenly, Aya announces, "I'm hungry!"

Soon the family is eating traditional Tatar food in one of the cafes on Baumana Street. They enjoy ELESH, ECHPOCHMAK and BELESH, which are baked pies made of chicken and beef mixed with potatoes, accompanied by salads and broths. They finish lunch with CHAK-CHAK, a honey based desert along with milk tea.

After seeing the center of Kazan, they ride slides, swim in indoor and outdoor pools, and visit a typical Russian sauna called BANYA in Riviera Aquapark.

Now it is time for George to do some work in the Ural Mountains. The family rents a car in Kazan, and after driving east and crossing the Volga and Kama rivers they reach their destination.

While George is busy collecting data for his study on the climate change and its effect on the flora and fauna in the Kapova Cave, Kate explores nearby areas with the kids in the Republic of Bashkortostan, a neighboring territory of Tatarstan.

After seeing the cave itself, which is also known as Shulgan-Tash, they spend their time collecting wild ZEMLYANIKA berries and watching birds in a nature preserve.

After camping in the wilderness of the Urals, the family arrives in Yekaterinburg, the 4th biggest city in Russia, named after Catherine the Great. "Dad, we are on the eastern side of the Urals now, right? Are we officially in Asia?" wonders Nick.

"Ekaterinburg stands right on the geographic border of Europe and Asia," his dad responds. "It was often referred to as the 'window to Asia' while Saint Petersburg was the 'window to Europe'."

"Today we are going to the Circus of Ekaterinburg and to a cafe where we will eat PELMENI, a traditional Russian version of dumplings that can be filled with meat, mushrooms or vegetables," Kate announces.

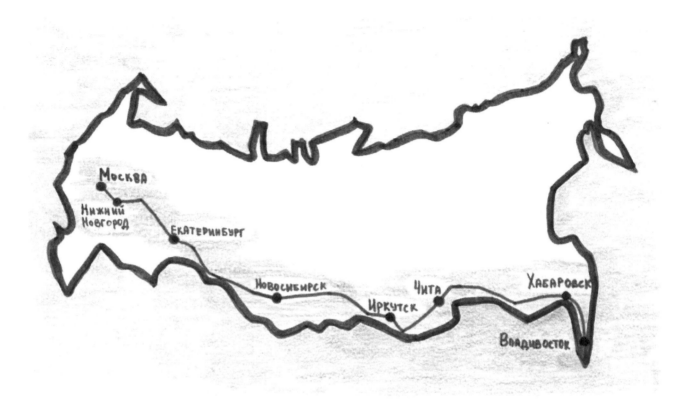

After the weekend, the four travelers purchase tickets and board a train on the Trans-Siberian Railway, a network of railroads connecting Russia's capital with the regions of the Far East.

The route between its beginning in Moscow and its end in Vladivostok is 9,258 kilometers (5,800 miles) long.

On the third day after boarding the train, the family arrives in Irkutsk, and after getting enough rest in the city they go on to Lake Baikal, the deepest lake in the world.

They take a boat trip and prepare for a multi-day hike on Great Baikal Trail together with other foreign travelers.

There are people from Germany and France in their group too, but Nick hears some English and says, "Hi! I am Nick and we are from the United States. What is your name? And from where are you traveling?"

"Hi! My name is Avery, and we are from the United States, too!"

The next morning all the children gather for breakfast around the fire to learn how to make a Russian style porridge called KASHA.

Later they explore the Barguzin Valley in Buryat Republic, another territory of the Russian Federation.

In the Barguzin River, which flows into Lake Baikal, Nick catches his first ever grayling, a fish with tall sail-like fins.

Then on the way to Ulan-Ude, the capital of Buryatia, they stop by a Buddhist Temple called Ivolginsky Datsan. Aya is looking at the building in amazement; she has never seen such a structure before.

"Dad, what is this?" she asks curiously.

"Do you remember seeing those buildings with crescents and crosses that represent either Islam or Orthodox Christianity? Well, this is one of the symbols of Buddhism. Buddhists follow the teachings of an enlightened Indian man known as Buddha who lived between the 6th and 4th centuries BC," responds George. "Hmm, ok! I still have many questions, but I want to see the statues first. I'll ask the questions later! Let's go!" exclaims Aya.

From Ulan-Ude, the family flies to the Kamchatka Peninsula. During the flight, the kids are looking out the window of the plane at the farthest eastern part of Russia's vast territory. They are following the flight map and see the Russian borders with Mongolia and China and the proximity of Russian Sakhalin Island to Japan.

George has another assignment and is meeting his colleagues in Petropavlovsk-Kamchatsky, the capital of Kamchatka Peninsula. Nick wants to see how his father conducts a research study, so he joins the group of scientists as they board a helicopter to fly to the Sedanka Spring Creek.

They camp by the river for several days, sleeping in tents. Nick sees bears, fish, and other wildlife while the team records their findings.

Meanwhile, Aya and her mother visit the Valley of Geysers, soak in hot springs and take a swim in the Sea of Okhotsk. "Mom, there are so many volcanoes here! Can we go closer to see one?" Aya asks.

"Your dad and Nick are coming back tonight and we will ask them if we can do that," promises her mother.

When Nick and his father return, the family goes on a guided tour to the Koryaksky Volcano. The hike up the mountain is not easy for Aya, and soon she rides in her child carrier on daddy's back. Everyone on the tour is fascinated with the majesty of Planet Earth after seeing this magnificent sight.

"Mom, do we have to fly all the way to Moscow now, before we can take a flight back home?" asks Nick. "That's a great question, son! No, we don't have to fly west. We will take a plane in Petropavlovsk-Kamchatsky and fly east to Anchorage, Alaska," his mother explains.

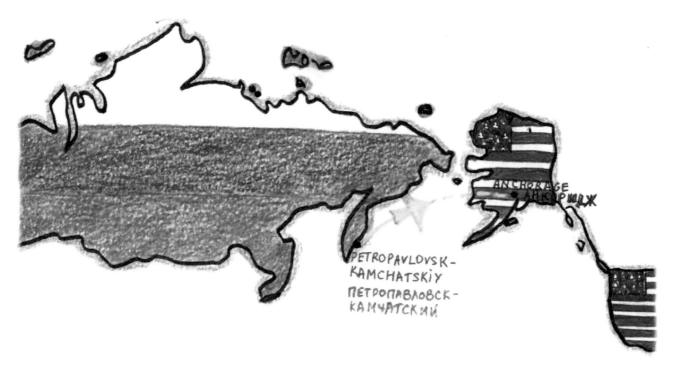

PETROPAVLOVSK-
KAMCHATSKIY
ПЕТРОПАВЛОВСК-
КАМЧАТСКИЙ

ANCHORAGE
АНКОРИДЖ

"We will be flying over the Bering Strait which separates Alaska from Russia," his father adds. "Alaska was a Russian colony in the past, but since 1867 it has been part of the USA."

"Are you serious?! We came to Russia crossing the Atlantic, and now we will be going to the States by flying over Pacific? We went all the way around the world! This is so exciting! I love traveling and seeing new things!" exclaims Nick.

"Me, too!" his sister excitedly agrees.

Five hours after boarding the flight in Kamchatka, the family lands in Anchorage, Alaska. They are filled with memories from their two-month-long trip to the largest country in the world.

Have you already read the first book from the series Nick and Aya Travel the World?

If not, check out Nick and Aya Travel to Argentina.

The story takes its readers first to Buenos Aires followed by Bariloche, where the family then starts their adventure driving a rented minivan throughout Patagonia. Children learn the names of existing plants, animals, fish, national landmarks and food items typical for Argentina. While following Nick and his sister Aya, the readers virtually visit a cave, a glacier, a bird sanctuary, lakes, streams and mountains.

They end their vacation at the largest waterfall system in the world and return home full of new impressions.

Recommended age: 5 and up.

Made in United States
North Haven, CT
01 December 2022

27622479R00027